Incredible
Insects

Claire Llewellyn

Heinemann Educational Publishers

Halley Court, Jordan Hill, Oxford OX2 8EJ

a division of Reed Educational & Professional Publishing Limited

Heinemann is a registered trademark of Reed Educational & Professional Publishing Limited

OXFORD MELBOURNE AUCKLAND

JOHANNESBURG BLANTYRE GABORONE

IBADAN PORTSMOUTH(NH) USA CHICAGO

First published 1998

02 01 00 99 98

10 9 8 7 6 5 4 3 2 1

British Library Cataloguing in Publication Data

A catalogue record for this book is available from the British Library.

ISBN 0 435 09651 6: *Incredible Insects* single copy

ISBN 0 435 09652 4: *Incredible Insects* 6 copy pack

Designed by M2

Printed and bound in the UK

Acknowledgements

Photos Andy Purcell / Bruce Coleman Ltd, page 5 top. P. Morris / Ardea London Ltd, page 5 bottom. Ardea London Ltd, page 7. Kjell Sandved / Oxford Scientific Films, page 9. Jane Burton / Bruce Coleman Ltd, page 10 top. John Clegg / Ardea London Ltd, page 10 bottom. Peter Steyn / Ardea London Ltd, page 11. Daniel Heuchlin / NHPA, page 15. M.P.L Fogden / Bruce Coleman Ltd, page 16. Gerald Cubitt / Bruce Coleman Ltd, page 17 top. Andrew J. Purcell / Bruce Coleman Ltd, page 17 bottom. Claudio Nuridsany and Marie Perennou / Science Photo Library, page 20 top. Alastair Macewen / Oxford Scientific Films, page 20 bottom and page 21 middle. Peter Parks / Oxford Scientific Films, page 21 top. London Scientific Films, page 21 bottom.

Illustrations / Mark Stewart (Wildlife Art Agency), title page and page 4. Roger Goringe (Garden Studio), contents page right and top, pages 6, 7, 9, 11 ,18 and 20. Mike Atkinson (Garden Studio), contents page left, imprint page bottom, pages 12 (except top left), 13 (except top left) and 21. John Butler (Ian Fleming and Associates), imprint page top and page 8. Alan Male (Linden Artists), pages 12 top left, 13 top left, 14, 15 and 19. David Wright (Kathy Jakeman Illustration), pages 16 and 17.

Contents

What is an insect?

An insect is an animal with three parts to its body and three pairs of legs. Many insects have long feelers called **antennae** on their head, and most of them also have wings. Insects are usually small, but in warmer parts of the world they can grow surprisingly large. The Indonesian giant stick insect, for example, grows to about 33cm long. It would just fit across this open book!

The body of an insect

Many insects look quite different from one another. Yet they all have the same body plan.

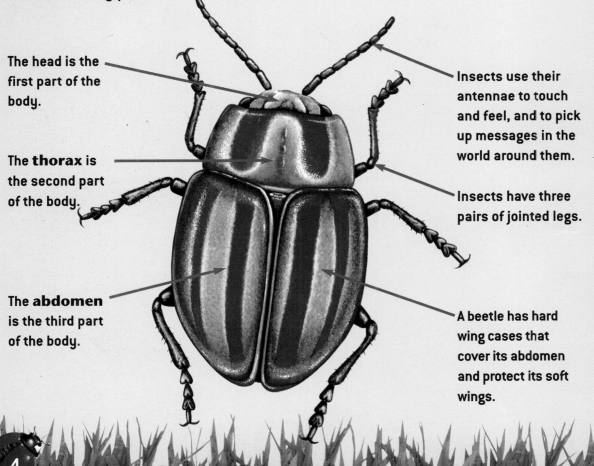

The head is the first part of the body.

The **thorax** is the second part of the body.

The **abdomen** is the third part of the body.

Insects use their antennae to touch and feel, and to pick up messages in the world around them.

Insects have three pairs of jointed legs.

A beetle has hard wing cases that cover its abdomen and protect its soft wings.

4

A hard case

Insects do not have bones. Instead, they have a hard case called the **exoskeleton** on the outside of their bodies. This protects their soft insides, just like a strong suit of armour.

This shield bug has a very clear exoskeleton. ▶

DID YOU KNOW?

Insects appeared over 300 million years ago, long before the first dinosaurs. Scientists know this because they have found fossils of insects in ancient rocks.

This is a fossil of a ▶ *dragonfly. The outline of its body and wings is clearly visible.*

Insect families

There are more than one million different kinds of insects in the world. Each kind is called a **species**. Scientists have examined the species and sorted them into groups.

There are about 30 different insect groups. The chart below shows seven of the most common groups. Each group has a special feature that makes it different from the others.

Insect groups

Beetle family
Insects with tough wing cases to protect their wings
Over 380,000 species
The largest insect group

Butterfly and moth family
Insects with wings that are covered by tiny scales
About 140,000 species

Bee, wasp and ant family
Insects with front and back wings that hook together
Over 100,000 species

DID YOU KNOW?

People who study insects are called **entomologists**. They travel all over the world to learn more about insects. Each year, they discover about 8,000 new species!

In this picture, an entomologist is catching insects. ➤

Fly family
Insects with one pair of wings
About 65,000 species

Bug family
Insects with a needle-like beak for stabbing and sucking up food
About 60,000 species

Grasshopper and cricket family
Insects with long bodies, leathery front wings and strong back legs
About 20,000 species

Dragonfly family
Insects with long bodies and two pairs of stiff wings
About 5,000 species

On the wing

Most insects can fly. This helps them to search for their food, and escape from danger. Insects' wings are soft and easily damaged. If they are torn, they cannot be repaired.

Taking off

A ladybird is a kind of beetle. Its delicate flying wings are hidden under tough wing cases.

 1 The ladybird crawls to the top of a stem.

2 It opens its brightly-coloured wing cases.

 3 It unfolds its flying wings, and beats them up and down.

4 Soon the wings beat so quickly that they lift the ladybird into the air.

Types of wings

Different insect groups have different types of wings.

A common wasp has two pairs of wings. The back pair is smaller than the front pair.

A butterfly has two pairs of wings that beat together.

A dragonfly has two pairs of wings. Each pair works on its own.

A house fly has only one pair of wings.

A butterfly's wings

Most insects have **transparent** wings with tiny veins. A butterfly's wings are different. They are covered by tiny scales that overlap like the tiles on a roof.

DID YOU KNOW?

- Flies beat their wings up to 1,000 times a second. That's what makes them buzz!

- About 300 million years ago, some dragonflies had a wing span of 70 cm. They were the size of seagulls!

A magnified photograph of the scales on a butterfly's wings.

Insect senses

Like all animals, insects need information about the world around them. They need to know whether there is food, a mate or an enemy near by. Insects gather this information with their senses, especially with their eyes and **antennae**.

Looking around

Insects have huge **compound eyes**. These are built up of hundreds of single eyes, or 'eyelets', each with its own tiny lens. Insects use the information from all the different eyes to produce a picture. Insects have a very wide view, but they see less clearly than we do.

Compound eyes

A dragonfly's huge compound eyes take up most of its head

This magnified photograph of a compound eye shows how the eyelets fit together. Some insects have up to 15,000 eyelets in each eye.

Antennae at work

Antennae are useful tools. Insects use them to touch and taste things, pick up smells and movements in the air, and sometimes even to hear. Antennae come in many shapes and sizes.

A bush cricket waves its long antennae to sniff out food.

A weevil is a type of beetle. Its antennae grow out of its snout.

A butterfly's slim antennae are club-shaped at the tip.

A cockchafer beetle fans out its antennae as it flies. They tell it which way the wind is blowing.

DID YOU KNOW?

Dung beetles have an excellent sense of smell. They can find a pile of fresh dung just 60 seconds after it has hit the ground!

Growing up

Young insects hatch out of eggs. They feed hungrily, shedding their skin as they grow. As insects get older, their bodies change shape. This process is called **metamorphosis**. In some insects metamorphosis happens slowly. In others it happens quite suddenly.

The lifecycle of a dragonfly

A dragonfly's body changes shape slowly.

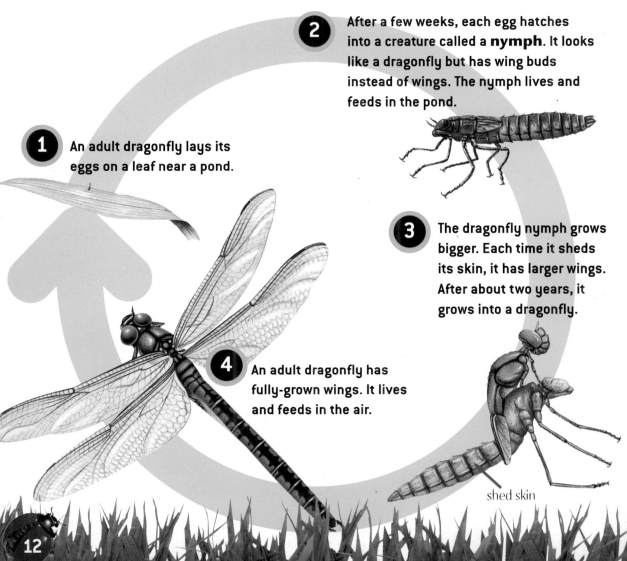

2 After a few weeks, each egg hatches into a creature called a **nymph**. It looks like a dragonfly but has wing buds instead of wings. The nymph lives and feeds in the pond.

1 An adult dragonfly lays its eggs on a leaf near a pond.

3 The dragonfly nymph grows bigger. Each time it sheds its skin, it has larger wings. After about two years, it grows into a dragonfly.

4 An adult dragonfly has fully-grown wings. It lives and feeds in the air.

shed skin

The lifecycle of a butterfly

A butterfly's body changes shape suddenly.

2 After about two weeks, the egg hatches into a tiny caterpillar. It looks nothing like a butterfly. The caterpillar feeds on the plant, and grows very quickly.

1 An adult swallowtail butterfly lays an egg on a plant.

3 About one month later, the fully-grown caterpillar makes a hard case called a **pupa**. Inside the pupa the caterpillar changes shape.

4 A few weeks later, an adult butterfly crawls out of the pupa and flies away.

Feeding

Insects feed on different kinds of food. Some insects feed only on plants. Others feed only on animals. Many eat anything that comes their way. Insects have different kinds of mouthparts to suit the food they eat.

Feeding on plants

Insects eat many different parts of a plant. Butterflies feed on the sugar-sweet nectar they find inside flowers. Aphids make holes in stems and leaves, and suck up the watery sap.

*A butterfly has a long, curly tongue called a **proboscis**. The insect uses it to suck up juicy nectar from flowers.*

proboscis

An aphid stabs plants with its sharp little beak, and then feeds on the sweet-tasting sap.

beak

Feeding on animals

Many insects feed on animals. Mosquitos drink the blood of living animals. Burying beetles feed on dead animals. They are like rubbish collectors, and clean up all the mucky waste.

jaws

mouthparts

▲

These burying beetles are using their sharp jaws to eat the flesh of a dead animal.

▲

A female mosquito has sharp mouthparts. She pushes them through an animal's skin, and sucks up a meal of blood.

DID YOU KNOW?

Only female mosquitos suck up blood. They need it to make their eggs. Male mosquitos feed on nectar instead.

Staying alive

Insects use all sorts of tricks to help them stay alive. They need to hunt for their food as well as defend themselves from their enemies.

On the attack

Insects have different ways of catching their prey.

*A flower mantis uses **camouflage** to catch a meal. It is so well hidden on a flower that it can easily ambush its prey. It pounces on insects and eats them up.*

An ant-lion larva hides at the bottom of a sandy pit. It flicks sand at ants to make them tumble into the pit, straight into the ant-lion's waiting jaws.

ant-lion larva

On the defence

Insects have lots of enemies, such as spiders, frogs and birds. Some insects hide from their enemies. Others try to frighten them away.

A leaf insect uses camouflage to survive. It looks just like a leaf.

A bombardier beetle frightens its enemies away. It makes a sudden 'bang', and shoots out a hot, stinging spray. Here a bombardier beetle is defending itself from a hungry shrew.

DID YOU KNOW?

The peacock butterfly has large eyespots on its wings. When it flashes its wings at its enemies, the 'eyes' scare them, and give the butterfly time to escape.

Living together

Some insects live in large family groups called **colonies**. A colony works as a team. Every member helps to build a nest, find food, fight enemies and care for the eggs and young.

Social insects

Ants, termites, wasps and honeybees all live in colonies. They are called social insects.

Honeybee

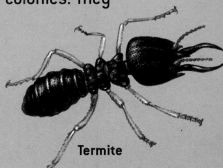

Termite

Ant

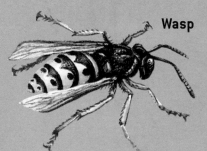

Wasp

A wasps' nest

Wasps build their nest out of thin sheets of paper. They make the paper themselves by chewing up tiny bits of wood.

> ## DID YOU KNOW?
> A wasps' nest is delicate and needs re-building every year. A bees' nest is made from wax. It is much stronger, and can last for 50 years .

How a wasps' nest is built

1 The queen wasp starts the nest on a wooden beam. She makes a small, round paper cap.

2 She makes some little cups called cells, and builds a case around them. She lays an egg in each cell.

3 The eggs hatch. The young soon grow into worker wasps. They help to build the nest. They work on the inside to tear down the old case and build lots of new cells.

4 More and more wasps hatch, grow and help to build the nest. In four months it is the size of a football with room for 10,000 tiny cells.

The inside of a wasp's nest

Insects in the home

Many insects like to live in our warm and sheltered homes. Most of the insects are so tiny that we cannot even see them. Every day, they feed on our food and on many other things our houses contain.

The housefly

Houseflies spread germs and disease. One moment, they are crawling around in the dirt; the next, they are on your sandwich. When a fly lands on food, it sicks up juices from its stomach, which dissolve the food and make it runny. The fly's mouthparts work like a sponge, and it uses them to suck up the dissolved food.

The furniture beetle

A furniture beetle's eggs hatch into tiny woodworm. They tunnel their way through furniture and beams, feeding on wood as they go. In time they can make a roof collapse.

The flea

Fleas feed on the blood of animals such as cats and dogs. They only feed on humans if they are very hungry.

The headlouse

Headlice like the warmth of people's heads. These tiny insects lay their eggs in our hair, and have extra-strong claws to hold on tight.

The dust mite

Swarms of house dust mites live in our homes. They feed on the tiny flakes of dead skin that we brush off every day.

Glossary

abdomen the back end of an insect's body

antenna (plural: antennae) one of a pair of feelers on an insect's head, which it uses to feel its way around and pick up messages in the air

camouflage the colours and markings on an animal which help it to blend in with its surroundings and make it difficult to see

colony a large group of animals that live together

compound eye an eye that is made up of many small eyes packed together

entomologist a scientist who studies insects

exoskeleton the hard casing on the outside of an insect's body

metamorphosis the change from a young insect into an adult insect (eg. from a caterpillar to a butterfly)

nymph the young stage of an insect such as a dragonfly, which changes slowly into an adult without making a pupa

proboscis the long tube-like mouthpart of the butterfly or moth, which it uses to suck up nectar

pupa the stage in an insect's life when it forms a hard case and changes into an adult

species a group of animals that are all the same kind and can breed together

thorax the middle part of an insect's body, between the head and the abdomen

transparent fine enough to see through

Index